"Allow life to unfold without urgent demand."
—Richard Rudd

"I was in training to be a woman without shame."
—Sandra Cisneros

Table of Contents

D

To all the boys I've loved before (that same old song)

You backed me up in half-light of green rooms,
made me watch our shadows intussuscept,
charmed me with false philosophies to cover mediocrity,
and set my body free, among other things, into deep woods.

You fed my insatiable appetite on floors littered with propaganda,
changed my status from girl to woman in the most uneventful way,
melted me with bedroom eyes while taking me at will, without protest,
and chased the nightmares into small hours of the morning.

You drove the sadness from the center of me,
filled yourself with what little I had to offer,
found a softness in me I had thought was long gone
and kissed my eyelids in the morning rain.

You walked a life with me laced in music and fallen hopes,
stole pieces of me that would never be returned,
shared me with your own lover without asking
and kissed my neck in dark empty theaters.

To all the boys I've loved before, I sing now
that same old song on the radio, one last time
before your memories are tucked away
like secrets of things imagined and unheard.

J

Nightgown

Those were the nights,
sneaking out of my apartment,
running down the alley
in bare feet and nightgown
escaping stories told to be with you;
to hear your voice
to whisper your brand
of lies in my ear,
all of which
I wanted to hear.

I liked you to violate me,
I liked the game
laced with stolen
secret glances.

We couldn't hate
each other as we confessed
to everyone. We had pieces
of soul locked in a box
secured from our own hands.

I loved those nights
now that they are gone,
those nights
filled with moonlit runs,
air-filled temptations,
cold water and smokes
on the porch.

We smiled then.
I miss that most.

Today

It feels like winter today
with dark skies closing in,
a clouded sarcophagus.

Teeth chatter standing outside
contemplating the warmth
of your fire.

I'll lay my head in your lap
thankful for the heat,
undeniably too happy that it
feels like winter today.

There Is No Stopping Time

Our life together
dissolved over a plate
of spaghetti you refused
to eat and my unwillingness
to console you.

We melded later that night,
passion consuming the bitterness,
our sad souls fitting into
one another like a complicated
puzzle constructed by meticulous
architects. Each moment was intense.

We lay there afterwards,
children huddled from a cold,
winter chill, like friends
in needy times, like a lover
who knows all there is to know.

We drifted to dream
hoping someday, somehow
we could stop the disintegration.

Jesus has dancing girls

Jesus, has dancing girls
and a cheesy used car salesmen
in his godly employ.

"Listen here folks," Cadillac man says
on center stage with heavenly gyrating nymphs,
"Jesus loves YOU more than your parents,
more than your children,
even more than your spouse."

My husband looks at me, sideways glance,
eyebrow raised as if to inquire
about my extra-marital affairs,

"With Jesus?" I reply out loud
laughing wildly, "Most definitely."

Roadside Dreams

I was half in love with ideas and a man
I'd once shook hands with and saw the future.

That future found us living check to check
in a ghetto on the outskirts of a racist city,
with our faces being the minority,
but with youth on our side
and a paved road ahead.

We believed nothing stopped love
and that love set to seed inside me
and multiplied into glory
that was never as sweet
the second time around.

We rolled the windows down,
sailed through the humidity
as I begged you to stop
so I could pick wildflowers—
Queen Anne's Lace, Chicory,
Mustard and California Poppy,
nothing more than pauper's gifts.

Bent in the field something faltered,
a vise grip squeezing me
and the earth plummeted all at once.

In the roadside station bathroom
I prayed to a God who had abandoned me
for the whole of my life,
I begged to let this be something
other than the truth.

I lost him there, both of them,
head resting on the cool
porcelain sink with arms
crossed, body doubled
and split. The subtraction
forever greater than the whole.

What I Have to Offer

This wet stain hovering
above the green stripes
on the sheets, cool to my flesh,
reminds me that I can still illicit
a reaction from you
that what I have to offer
still excites, still drives
your sex to rise against
the coup of domestication.

Meant to be Broken

Driving down the highway
into a rising fog thick from the river,
and I feel stuck inside my brain
thinking of the force your will pushes me with,
how it punishes me into humility.

Moving around the bend faster than the limit,
grinding random rules between my teeth,
their acrid taste scares me because
I cannot get enough, and the sun bursts
sideways through the density
turning everything white.

I feel your hand, cool and smooth,
softly wiping away the condensation of my fear.
Your skin wet with the heaviness of me,
with the residue of my emotional explosions,
rabid dog obscenities, and lack of control.

You touch my chaos
to your mouth
and it taints
the waters between us.

Fallout

Noise from your mouth
drifts into my airspace
like shards of glass in my ears.

I cannot find the words
                to tell you the truth.

You like it like that, you
and me, alone with your face
like a mirror, forcing me
to watch this internal   suffering.

You exist in a selfish
capsized world, locked
in the basement,   going
                under
a process of devolution

and smile as the pain settles
like fallout on my face—
s m u d g e d and dirty
twisting in the wind.

Folded

Calculated barbs hook my flesh
with meditated precision
as accusations are made
about taking that which isn't mine,
of tasting forbidden fruits

His face burns with smugness
waiting for the one steely point
to fold me neat into his palm again,
the one weakness to make me forget
each slight and condensation of character
spread over half my lifespan.

I sit here now a smooth stone,
blood emptying into the gray center of his fire,
damp and still and cool to the touch.

The Sting of Absolutes

Hands run over glass
searching for imperfections,
the bubble beneath the surface
is enough to pierce your
face with a smile.

You must know
its presence instinctively
to see it with eyes closed.

Your tongue had to have
tasted the other but once
to know the feel of it.

A sting of absolutes
sends you in directions seeking
only that which is broken,
that which might never heal,
to hold between your fingers.

Sweet Memory

The air shifts
when the door opens
creeping down the hallway
on the jangle of your keys,
on the creaking of the stairs
under the weight
    of your displeasure.
It moves around me
tentative, seeking
its grip coiling
around my throat
until air is just
a sweet memory.

Solitude

I never imagined
that silence shared equal space
with banality,

that one could lead to another,
that one could grow
from the seed of the other,

that the hours of our solitude
with no words
to pass between us

would become our demise
when it had been our salvation.

4 Cents An Acre

I stand in line at the wrong window
for a long time, shifting weight
from left to right, satchel heavy with poetry
and melancholy, both unrelated.

The woman behind the glass looks
at me with feigned sympathy as I request
papers for uncontested divorce. She tips
her head to the next plexi barrier.

I thought that statement would give me
a sense of liberation: uncontested divorce,
but spoken slowly and echoing off
county clerk office walls only says

someone was willing to give me up
without a fight. She hands me the stack
gingerly, thick and neatly stapled, and
it feels dirtier than the Louisiana Purchase.

Before I make the door, I stare at the cover
with its tidy blue state seal knowing
I'd soon break promises I meant to keep.

Complications of Love

My day is made up
of little cuts and digs
drizzled with rubbing
                              alcohol
He is oblivious
to the way it stings me,
damages me,
even when told.

He is blinded
by the parameters
of the fence
he's built
around my love,
around me
to keep me from
                              moving
too far out of mediocrity.

Fading

Sorrow cascades
over our candlelit faces
after the decision is made
that we have loved too much,
or not enough
to hold us fast
to the truth of together.

Whispers Something About Irony

I fold the laundry
in between loads of dishes
as you make lists in the air
ticking off items collected over the years.

Placing them in neat piles, short and haphazard,
you realize most everything
is mine by default.

The sound of our child
singing in the background,
clothes tumbling in the dryer,
the cat under foot wondering
when the tension will be gone,
and when I will resume scratching his ears.

You drag me around the apartment
as if you were showing me the place,
pointing out features. Each room is scanned
with two sets of eyes placing invisible tags
of ownership until the tour ends
back in the living room.

You notice the clock,
given to us at our wedding,
stopped telling proper time
and mention the Swedish Love Knot
that unraveled years ago.

And under your breath,
as you go to smoke,
you whisper something about irony.

Operative

He left in winter
one week after
everyone makes
resolutions they
never intend to
keep, and the sun

on the moving van
glass hints at deception
as the air reminds
me this event
is growing icicles
in my newly freed heart.

I watch him drive
away, fingers holding
the blinds apart, spying
on the calculated
selfishness that lead me
to this moment,

the idea that change
is always about bravery,
as it wraps tightly around my
defeated and slumped
shoulders. In real time
I am finally alone.

Apples and Cinquains

Sitting next to him in the cusp
of what would have been
sixteen years of life spent
in each other's company,
I heave a breath that cuts the room.

Our backs hunch over
sitting in the tiny blue chairs
built for small people
as we listen to our progenies
academic achievements.

The teacher looks through
the painful silence between us
and I find myself counting the puffs of oxygen
coming from the tank neatly strapped to her back
to distract me from the truth of it all.

At the end, we stare at the pile
of drawings and stories,
the culmination of our combined seeds,
trying to decide what fragments of her
we cannot bear to part with.

As I walk to my car alone,
I look sideways and see him there
in his seat, sun hitting the windshield
and his face is twisted as if crying.
Part of me wants to knock on the window
and simply say, "I'm sorry."

But I know that would somehow
never be enough,

so I keep walking
with the sound of gravel under my feet.

Unfirm Gelatin

I used to be a lover of believing,
a wanter of more, but that was anyone's capability,
and I let it make me reckless with skin and lust,
fulfilling typical credos of American impatience.
The hunger for instant gratification
proof positive we are all byproducts
of the ME generation, swimming in our own filth.

But I loved you then, with a certain simplicity,
believed we'd be forever, wrapped in a school girl's longing
for normality and safety.
But my naiveté painted a bull's eye across my chest
and men drew back their deep desires,
releasing taut strings impressed into fingers.
The wind of the hunt lightly blowing over their lips
as arrows tipped in hunger hurtled from the bow.

These faded remembrances cling to my fingers,
sticky with unfirm gelatin, and my prints mark them
with an understanding that pictures can be mortal enemies
filling the mind, retrieving pains and joys,
as if they were books cataloged in a library.
The dates of my life in the hands of Dewey
with my collection growing daily.

I realize now, standing in the kitchen,
that I loved you most then when your great distance
from my heart could not touch me,
where your impact, however great or small,
could not physically change me.

I was free.
I was imprisoned.
I am free, again.

Faltered Exchange Through the Doorway

I want to punch things—
    his face, our failed
marriage, his inability to live
      now, his incessant need to fumble
        backwards in loop, his voice
      a skipping record.

I want to scream obscenities
into the phone, decimate
what's left of him, knock
him further into the ground
so he can't resurrect Lazarus
again and again and again,
each time voiding another
good memory from our crumbled
          union.

But I cannot
    I will not
    I won't.
        Instead I breathe deeply
        and imagine myself
           encased in the ribs
           of Gandhi.

E

Fragile

Women spend their time
whittling away his heart, soft as soap,
each tender word slicing curls of lye
and fragrance so easily melted
with careless, warm tears.

It is their American sensibility,
inbred ideals of wasting, of unending
abundances, of grasses greener in another pasture
while the seeds of his heart prepare
to germinate with only the thought of a gentle touch,
so willingly cultivated by glances ripe
with desires promised.

But these women do not understand
the chemical composition
of something as fragile as soap, as love,
something so simple and pure with its powers
to cleanse all that is tainted, to hold them upward
into rebirth, into the sun that rises
above the morning fog
hanging heavy over their lids.

Olly, Olly Oxen Free

This forest is thick with haves and have nots,
heavy with could be's, drenched
in the evenings lingering dreams.

I see him around the tree
hiding and holding his breath,
shushing the sound of his heart beating
louder than fists swung in a rage.

He finds that place where it quiets
and limbs relax into the bark
and sounds have silence
under their tongues.

And I cannot stand to watch it
so easily attained, this restraint
and knowing of concepts
that have always been
my crosses to bear,
with their heavy hands
upon me, no intentions
of sharing the burden.

So I leave him there
backed into his tree,
in his sounded silence,
his miraculous resolutions
of heart, and slip into the dark.

In answer to all things green

I wound myself around his winter,
huddled close to warm that which froze inside him,
gentle at first then stronger, not knowing the cost.

I spied on the darkness of his mind,
that place above the heart surrounded
by dying springs and perpetual transitions
from autumn to winter; seasons of distraction
that consumed him with their return.

And it was his tenacity for words
all shapes and sizes, of all languages
formed into tiny perfections
of the highest quality of love,
that hooked me closer to his pain,
stitched me in until it was mine too.

I fell into him uninvited,
made a place within his empty garden
dense with overgrowth, neglected
until paths barely visible.
I pulled at the weeds on hands and knees,

clearing and clearing

until fingers were stained green,
until there was something lush and hidden revealed
in a laugh like a song to me,
something pure and sweet.

He could not contain it
and I could not ignore it,
so I pulled and pruned anticipating

more laughter, more words to consume
my own growing pains.

He built fences wooden and uneven,
soft reminders of boundary
I was too blind to see.
They were for saving him,
pushed back my hands
from touching the small
fragment of heart
still beating on its own.

And night came to the garden.
Under moonlight I sat in that first clearing,
the place where laughter started
where smiles were conjured
and still found it green, overgrowing again.

No sun's light could kill it.
Not even my brightness could close the scar
dug deep into its earth with her hand
touching the rim of its canyon.

I allowed the salt from my eyes
to fall onto it, onto the green, onto their laughter
because it was all
I could think to do.

Rivalry

I
slept in,
awakening
to soft sunshine,
silence.

I
stretched,
moving dreams
from deep in
muscles.

Your
words linger
still, haloed loosely
around ears,

> a touch of gold,
> a sleight of hand,

that
rivals Midas,
for every pound
he's worth.

The Folk House

I.
Rusted bars creak when your right hand pushes open the gate,
your other, warm and firm in the valley of my back; a gentleman
of the first degree. The gesture at once quickens my heart.
We laugh nervously in the long, dark corridor with its catacomb
silence, and my clicking heels on the Spanish tile ring loud.
The walls rough beneath my fingers, an earthen Braille,
its beauty only grasped in this temporary blindness.
The tunnel opens easily into a courtyard, wooden trellis crowned
and dripping with wisteria, the color reminds me of the lilac still in my hair,
plucked deviously from a stranger's tree, when you said you'd never
  smelled it.

II.
I listen to the lilt of your voice making small talk, letting you go on,
knowing very well that you hate it, but you sense it will draw me out
  into this night;
this first mingling in the world without being caught inside the box.
We smoke, inhaling deep the clouded sky heavy with complaint,
the flower's mixed perfumes, the chatter of friends, and the lingering smell
of our excitement, still fresh on the skin. I look up as the first drops
  descend,
the stars distant memories tonight; my life changes with each breath,
so fast I am spinning, and then all is quiet: your voice, the city, the
  people,
and I catch you watching me, smile spreading like a disease.

III.
You let me hold your hand beneath the table, the room lit
with white Christmas strands around the makeshift stage
and the whisper of *coup de foudre* taking my breath by surprise.
Closer, fire dances in votives by way of ghosts let in
through the high window, making kaleidoscope women behind

the soft brown bottles of Weston's, sweating rings onto the
  tabletop,
as the singer's voice shocks the air around us all.
We are captured in the church of his piano,
his voice the heaven we can't bring ourselves to believe exists,
and when he reaches the pinnacle, there is silence.

A Bee in the Belfry

You are a monk on the bench in the garden blessed by a god
neither of us believe in. Your belly a great rising and falling
of intuition as the faint perfumes from Yucca and Oxlip
float into your mouth on the easy breaths that come in half sleep,
and I a bee amidst the stems and petals, adventuring out
several feet at a time reporting back colors, whorled leaves,
and densely tangled ground cover to your deaf ears.

A benevolent smile peels your lips, eyes close in
the winking summer light dancing minuets
across the bridge of your nose until it finds me still
and silent in the world's greatest perfection.

I come to rest on the worn wood beside you,
leaving no space for air between us.
Our warming damp skins mingle,
ribs touch in rhythm to the raven's call;
your arm rests over my shoulder like moth wings
as the belfry comes alive, scattering vibrations through the blue.

My lungs hold their breath, feel yours continue
even and sweet, then release in time to meet
your bones that cage the dove, burning quiet.

You speak at once about bodies buried at our feet.
Their gift the flowers, wild and entangled,
growing from the bone dust of pious men.

I knew then,
I loved you.

Relinquished

We are salmon to spawn,
upstream through the five o'clock
merger filled with gray suits and cell phones,
as they let the automatons loose
on Oxford Street.

Here it is, London, its ideals
leached from books and travel guides,
all set into the grooves of my face; the decline
comes in thinking it is nothing more
than a squat NYC, wrapped in Olde World charm.

Your hand, warm in the evening chill,
rests on the back of my neck. The insurgent's
send you left of center, your fingers squeeze
into flesh in silent desperation.

We cross Oxford, near blind into sunset,
down a cobblestone road lined with smells
of shops and foreign restaurants, their air
a temptation we can't resist.

The tiled tables of moon and stars, paired
with the smell of hummus and Turkish coffee,
lend us shelter in the ever fading day. It is
surreal and defeating and life would never be the same.

Three for Tea

13 rooms fashioned in a time machine,
the relationship between magic and beauty building
until we collapse on the curved wooden bench,
golden slatted tree hearts carrying our weight,
facing Picabia's transparencies; eyes twitching then closed.

You tumble at last with face pinned to the glass
admiring Duchamp's chess set and his headiness
to give it all up for the game, moving pawns
through invisible patterns garnered in both minds,
ten steps ahead of time and space.

We emerge from the end of the tunnel into splintered light, its
    sudden lift
at once weary and heavy, pushing us down the escalator
through color blocked art we'd never witness. Descention
    brings
silence, no words equaling the imprints now in cells.
Our bodies part directions at the bottom.

I find you leaning over the rail outside the doors,
the glass towering above you, monolithic, and the fag
in your hand souring the air, the smoke pulls me closer.
I dream of suffocating the images, tweezing each color and form
from between sluiced gray matter with precision.

We curl our chests over together, watch relatives struggle
to push their fat, crippled kin up steep ramps from the
    underbelly.
The pompous rapid language of French pre-teens, intermittent
    with laughter,
tells how unsettled they are in their skins; how we all fit that
shame in one lifetime or another.

Our elbows touch point-to-point, inhaling and then out
love still molding and shaping its way onto blank canvas;
colors being chosen carefully, meticulous to a fault,
because some things cannot be erased.

The Lucky Toothpaste

We are the
4 am
morning bathed in cricketed silence, still darkness
before moon and sun have changed positions.

The steam billows under the door while you roll
into the imprint of my body in the sheets next to you
to breathe in our moments of sleep together.

In the slab of light, I stand naked and damp
watching this sweetness capture my heart.
I crawl in from the foot of the bed to lie next to you,
not wanting the inevitable.

Your fingers slide down my back to the swell
of my buttocks before allowing me to permeate
your very flesh while I taste your mouth, while I fly one last time.

It is a slow ride to the airport, the road curved and lined
with stones, the Celtic music mingling with the air from
the window rolled all the way down. I can smell myself
on your fingers and I kiss your palm, knowing.

We stand by the lighted sign in the lobby listening
to the low grumble of early morning travelers, espresso machines,
and the purr of taxis when automatic doors open.

You kiss me there like a lover; kiss me like I never existed.
Trails of silver run down my cheek as you walk away,
the words I want to tell you so badly
stuck firmly in my throat. Around the bend you come again,

hands cupping my face and pouring into me

a feeling of weakness and desperation as your thumb
runs the length of my lip and you are gone.

What summer tells me (whispered in my ear)

"Watch me! Watch me!" they shout
as they jump foot long into crystal water,
competing for attentions of skills remembered
from the summer passed.

I was a netted mermaid then,
beneath the surface, with waves
ricocheting from blue to blue
and lapping against 5's, three times,

remembering I had not begun
to think of you as more than a poem
I read somewhere, still anonymous
as the ocean I never thought I'd span.

Now, my face is upturned to the same sky
we both warmed our skins in weeks ago,
the grass holding my head, and I
holding yours in the crook of my hip.

Your fingers gently stroking the rise
of my calf, mine tracing the ink
resting in your arms, the permanently
impermanent remembrances of other things.

And this is so alive to me,
watching the children do flips
in man made waves and me ready
to swim back across the sea.

The Silenced Fan

It is the crest of 5am
when rough-throated garbles
of the rooster's crow weakly
filter up through a minted dawn
on the day of the Lord.

Sparrows call the light no one else can see,
tell relatives on the crisp pointed maples
and heady oaks about the slithering bounty,
silver trails lead from a nocturnal feeding
on the tender folded flowers in the bean patch.

House finches and mourning doves heed the tale,
twitter then coo in swirled feathers, the dawn
lighting iridescent wings that hover over
fat, homeless snails inching their getaway
by the night's last true moments.

Across the yard where new highway construction has halted,
shadowed machines on the banks
lumber as ancient beasts, iron dinosaurs
with heads rising above red-tipped leaves
chilled by the solemn beginning of autumn's breath.

The rooster calls again and brings notice
to the shimmer through the blinds, a burning white disc
whose beams trick the old cock
into dreams laced with coming dawn
and cracked corn spread around the dirt.

My fingers split the dusty slats to see the moon smile,
hear her whisper your name like a mantra
until it finds its way between the fan blades

gently turning as if lifted by wind. It coaxes me
to the shelter of quilted covers
where warm child limbs ease me back to sleep.

Dividing the flesh of an over-ripe tomato

There are similarities of nature
between she and I,
two women in love, one now and one no more;
same letters of alphabet and country of birth
(though the breadth of the land separated us),
dark glasses on pale faces
and ink that flows from fingers to page.

There is, of course, the manner of meeting;
the holiday and my uncanny desire to go
where memories all have her face
tattooed in the air, without knowing.

And I catch myself making excuses,
inviting the universe into the parlor where we sit,
to try and erase the distress growing beneath my tongue.
And you shrug it aside as an oddity
that needs no attention,
though we both know it gets plenty.

Ruminating in the kitchen over these facts,
tracking water on the floor
as lettuce drips from the rinse,
and thinking of her still,
as my knife forcefully divides the flesh
of an over-ripe tomato;
a faint smile erupts at the crisp sound
of English cucumber falling into slices on the board,
and thoughts about similarity and conjecture
and everything in its place at the right time
meet me at the counter.

The plausible notion that you stumbled

upon her first, misguided by same initials,
same country, pale skin and dark glasses
makes me wonder if it were me you had been looking for.
But we shall not know this until birds
take flight over open waters; until trees
give their sweet breath to the wind.

But from this view,
over my mountain of salad,
with the dressing making Pollack impressions,
I take the first bite of us thinking,
she and I are nothing alike.

The cat hides under the chair

Sometimes it is hard to love
you when the wind rushes
beneath my dress and the
skeletons of hills illuminate
what we already know.

Sometimes it is hard to love
you in the silence of this
room, its roar the only music,
save the savage world
beating on the screen of the window.

Sometimes it is hard to love
you as the tea goes cold
and still in the cup, when
the heart is lit
by a single fading candle.

Sometimes it is hard to love
you under the weight of the sky
falling like anvils to the ground,
under a night-cursed loneliness
of empty arms and breath.

Sometimes,
it is hard to love you.

hollow

we are a tangible child's pose
twisted unto ourselves
   in the bottom of the shower
hot water scalding
old hides into scarlet costumes.

we are the pain
creeping into joints without remorse,
   the pulling of muscles flexed
beyond intention, the subtle tightening
a warning to us all.

we are soon an empty shell
pink and new
   found on unformed particles of glass
potentials deep and tonal if only our fingers
could release it to the sea.

we are nothing save the loose flesh
stretched over sinew and long bones;
   human lorica, segmented
until returned to the earth a burrowed stillness,
slivers of magic found in the dead of night.

The scent of roses and coffee

We are equal in magnitude,
yet opposite in nature,
nothing more than a flux of energy
through a closed surface,
the sum of us equaling zero
stretched over continuous loops.

The line of me pours into you
as your hand touches the place
where the line of you had been,
keeping law intact, not disturbing
that which cannot be broken
or created by the downfall of man,
but it is that,
which just simply
Is.

D

How to save a life

You tell me you love me
under the spotlight of a small gooseneck reading lamp.
I feel you crawl onto the crisp sheets,
bed dipping under your weight as you
settle in beside me and whisper my name.
I roll over from my book feeling the heat
from your skin burn me, the look on your face
nearly as intense, and enough to make me hold my breath.

I feel your heart beating furiously on my elbow
as if some piece of your father's ghost
is trying to keep tempo with sticks worn smoother
than marble. This is a tune he won't quite catch.

And you speak the words I wasn't expecting to hear
after such a short time together; my own heart
rushing to the scene of the crime, wanting above all
other things to be able to love you back, to see
the light creep into your eyes whenever I enter the room,
but I can't be that close to the fire.
I can't put all of myself into your gentle arms
when I am not worth more than a broken China doll.

Tears roll down the square of thrown light on my cheek,
my mouth betraying its orders, the guardian asleep
at the gate, and I hear them fall into the air knowing
you need to hear me say it, knowing at that moment

my heart
felt the whole of it
burning into us both.

Sleight of hand

She gives you a bowtie
fashioned in primary colors, edges rough
and leaves the room; the door finds
its familiar click and release
when her small hand lets it go.

On our stomachs, we watch the rain
entertain the pavement, two fat crows
dance around in the gathering water
that washes the dirt away from this
monument that stands between us.

The smell of clean air touches you
as the tiny hardened clay turns over in your fingers,
the sweet gesture spreads like fire. I lay
my head on your shoulder, feel it vibrate there
in the skin, some brief encapsulated magic.

I am no barber

I cut your hair in the narrow kitchen
intent on the clippers buzz
purring softly in my palm, fingers
vibrating while speakers let out
a howl beyond the crowd, slant
perched on the lips of Waits
that you overlook for the sake
of a haircut and a view.

I am no barber and we both know this
having shared stories of demon coifs
given to my brother before picture day
two years in a row that incensed my mother.
They did not lack creativity as much
as they lacked pure skill and notion of angles.

You taste the anticipation of my fingers
brushing over the bristles on your crown,
how I gently fold over each ear to claim
escaped convicts and derelict marauders;
you wait for me to measure tangents
to make imposed hairlines; you wait for me
to stand between your legs with skin
so close you can smell the faint air of my ancestry.

Your hands dance with temptation, steal
kisses through cotton, stroke the rise of my
thigh or leave fingers to rest in the tender
cradle behind my knee; you read my breathing
like a well worn book, binding frayed and
rapidly declining but familiar. I feel the pulsing
of your neck when I brush the hair away. We
both smile unseen secrets.

Interplay

All night I worked, came home
to find you huddled on my sofa,
gray hoodie covering your head,
blankets pulled neatly under the chin.

Your feet hung over the edge
of the sage green arm.

You didn't hear my keys
jangle in the door, and all these years alone
gave me an internal stealth.
I stood there smiling, unknown.

The long night's ingrained lines
dissolved into softness.

You startled when I touched your forehead,
eyes darted and adjusted
in shocks of dilated hazel
until you remembered you were here,

in this house permeated with love,
ready to fill your empty pockets.

Oasis

After a night filled with torrent dreams,
my head caught barrel rolling
in tubular waves close to the ocean floor,
I awake to hieroglyphics
on your ceiling scripted in sunlight.

It is a strange language,
transitory and threaded with arced
light. It is written as if Urim
and Thummim has come
to show the way, to lay down
omens in which to follow.

We lie next to each other silent
and I still feel the depth of your reach,
the pulsing connection both primal
and tender, laced with underestimated
importance. Two lives make one
for a handful of moments, changing fates.

My eyes close as you trace the edge
of my shirt, skin still warm with sleep.
You make a map for this caravan—
plodding camels and heavy silence,
sun and wind and dreams of water
until your fingers find the oasis.

I meet you there, at this new place
where life turns and twists with easy
agitation and words become more felt
than spoken, where glyphs on the wall
move mountains and satisfy kings.

Year One

You dragged the mattress into the living room,
citing how insomnia has crept into every Sunday
of your life and how white noise somehow
soothes the beasts in your head
to rest, just enough to sleep.

At first I felt internally resistant, struggling
with lights flashing in pixilated repetition
around the dark room, each sound
from the television a knife
running along my nerves.

I felt your body crawl over mine, listened as you
placed "We Were Soldiers" into the tray of the player,
and then settle down beside me again.
I lay there still resisting the noise,
but as it continued, I softened.

We watched the first major conflict in the Vietnam war
and sorrow rolled down my cheeks silently
as young men took their deaths so afraid
and unsure, knowing this was once my father
in Vietnam and your father in Korea.

So there we lay on our anniversary, bodies locked
together in something deeper than we could
have imagined a year ago, *I could have never
been born* pounded through me as you
wiped tears and allowed my heart

to break, understanding
the repercussions
of war torn
childhoods.

Out to Sea

Hours after his sex
is gone from mine,
I still feel him there—
a resolute humming
with flesh pink and swollen.

We ride down the highway
to the beach in spring,
a notion we never
considered to be love,
but it is laden with it

not realizing it until now
in the cool ocean breeze, that
what we faced last year, in
our hats and scarves, watching
ships come in that we'd found
something worth keeping.

Simple

Love is as simple
as the three of us
lying sideways

over an inflatable
mattress on silky
earthen sheets

making guesses
on history and testing
the strength of knowledge.

Modern Short Stories

I cling to him in the night, a creeping
diurnal vine wrapping tendrils blindly
with fear imprisoned in petals,
anchored at his waist; a silent weed
internally bound in childlike myths.

The air in my lungs is thin
as if I climbed to the apex
of a mountain I was never meant to scale;
love, snow capped and infamous, looms
just in reach. He is sturdy, lets me belay

from his strength and knowing, a belief,
never mentioning my weakness
aloud, or gesturing my blatant cowardice
in the space between us,
and shows me the meaning of trust.

Increasing

I am bathed in the storm's electricity,
in its wet, pink musings
and I think about the hour passed
before and your low whisper in my ear;
erratic thunder kissing the hills.
The folds of my sex all too familiar
with your fingerprints and the velvet
texture of your tongue
always increasing and increasing
the architecture of my body.

Shifting Universes

I had realized I loved him
all along, and told him so,
but we had not seen the others face
until this moment.

My legs slung on either side of his,
knees settling into the creases
of the couch, the wood creaks
with a new shifting universe created.

He is warm with sleep
and our arms wrap around
each other, his head on my chest,
my lips on his crown, hearts thumping.

We stay like this, saying nothing,
because it was all being said.

He takes my hand, leads me
to the bedroom and undresses me.
He smiles at my nakedness, something
sweet and devilish at once,
and lays me on the bed, stomach down
with skin chilling in the air, waiting for him.

Delicate and feathery his fingers begin
at the ankle, massaging and exploring
each muscle on the atlas of my body
only stopping when my fingertips are found.

I feel human and alive.
I cannot resist the thought
of him inside me any longer,

and pull him into a kiss.

We fit together easily, our pleasure
effortless as we transcend space
and run rings around the moon,
time passes as if time does not exist.

Breaths stutter until even,
until we are again without pretense.

Gasoline Skin

I morph into
a different person
when he touches
my skin
lifting me
out of myself—
fingertips ablaze
on gasoline skin.
In full burn,
he puts me out
with his mouth.

After the party, standing in the rain

Today the rain has washed away that woman's
face done in chalk on the pavement
while I spoke to you that afternoon weeks ago.

I can still see her like a ghost,
hair pulled back in a loose bun
at her neck with tendrils at her ears.

I had plans for her, plans for retouching
the wisps of hair curled round, kissing her cheek,
plumping the bottom lip and shining the eye.

But life is messy and it gets cleared
when the universe sees fit to do it.
And I am surprised by how little it took
to clean the palette of its dust, leaving
no trace on the surface of its existence.

But the sun has burned it in
to the palm of my hand, into my retina
and I can still see the curve of her forehead from here.

Every Time You Go

I lay down naked between the sheets
stalling my shower and a play date
I didn't arrange, thinking about how little
I'll see you in the upcoming months.

Your smell is on my pillows and I bury
my face inside contemplating a second
chance at love I didn't deserve.

The fan blows in the next room, challenging
the volume of the TV, cartoons reminding me
of my duty to be like other moms and socialize,
but I'd rather lay here enveloped by Egyptian cotton

staring at my gray, gloomy paradise
trundled under rain, through slatted blinds,
than dip my toes in the pools of average people.

Here Dreams Gather

We drive in opposite directions,
each mile marker putting more space
between our bodies than I like.

The Grey Goose tops the first hill,
her engine humming sluggishly
at the incline grade.

At the apex, I am decimated
by the valley snaking through
the Catskill Mountains;

hills covered with new leaves
unfurling in greens only Mother
can create or name.

It is not yet lush, this valley,
but the promise is given
in semi-fore and sun flare.

Clouds are thick like cotton
layered as a nest with blue
above and silver lining below.

This always reminds me of you,
this valley of the Five Nations,
that always brings you closer to me,

closer to stolen glances and kissed
fingertips; closer to mornings
risen in the safety of arms,

to moments passed without
worry or wonder, closer to knowing
the meaning of truth.

Millbury Night

The sky has metabolized
into the blue of summer night
and the lights flip on in the field unnoticed
over the carnival sounds, but I see them
flare against the dark... those Friday night lights
you have seen so many times before.

And we stand like islands
amidst the swirling rides
and bustle of children
ready for more dizziness
anticipating fireworks; our
own anticipation heavy
and brimming but never
overflowing—it comes close
but settles sweeter and deeper
never dissipating in the wind.

Off Guard

His sock falls out of the dryer
and my heart beats quicker.
I think, *has it been that long
since I have seen something
of a man's mixed in with colorful
panties and tiny kid shirts?*

It tricks me into thinking
he is here, somewhere
in the next room with book
cradled in hand, succumbed
to short story classics—lulled
by the quiet filtering through

                              the windows.

I catch glimpses of him,
now and then, when the light
moves across the ceiling, or the room
is persecuted with stillness.
And then he flees as quickly
as he arrived, and leaves me
standing in front of an open machine,
heat clinging to the hem of my skirt
with one sock against my chest.

These days continue

The sun burns the left side of my face,
and the wind follows cooling the skin slightly
pushing a loose hair across my nose, tickling it.

Marley on the radio sings about Jammin'
as I peer over the laptop
at delicate blushed tulips and blue flags
unfurling in light; tiger lilies wait to explode
and I think of you sitting at the table with me.

Our silence would be comfortable
with hands reaching across the space between,
fingers touching like feathers.

Love is as easy as that one movement,
            easy as spring through paned windows,
            easy as the cat at our feet,
            easy as summer music,
or as easy as fresh faced flowers tilting towards heaven.

Yes, I think of you now,
here in this moment sharing life and breath,
holding hands in the afternoon.

The Seamless Gate

He leans forward
tripoding his bulk
on poetry and empty
beer cans. The air
vibrates from his lungs
into the bones of his ribs.

It is trapped confusion.
It is suffocated dreaming.
It is relinquished hope.

He grabs the words
as they are handed to him,
lays them gently
next to the water
sweating on the table.

The words keep coming
like machine gun fire
over stagnant air, from
the writer's mouth.

We all go to war
with that in our pockets.

A Handful of Days

Our bodies are framed in the bathrooms
unlit doorway, embraced, with my tears
spilling over onto your navy blue polo
with "coach" embroidered in gold
over your heart, where my hand lies.

We are surrounded by reflections;
the large mirror holds two lovers
stealing as quiet a goodbye as can be
mustered. The hall mirror gleams
with my daughter's sweet face

filled with desperate need
for my life to be normal and steady.
Your voice whispers into the seam
of my shirt, warm breath on my neck,
how we are always together

despite distance, how we have what most
never find in a lifetime of lifetimes,
and this makes me cry harder knowing
I have finally found it—love and longing—
that is never in my grasp

for more than a handful of days.
The leaving feels like a simmering death
until two weeks later when I am resurrected
by your hands wrapped around my face,
lips warm on my forehead, blessing us once again.

The Scene of the Crime

I saw myself as I must
have been these last 10 years,
cold and alone, while lying on
the Mexican blanket listening to old tyme
fiddlers jamming in the far tent;

he rose from the makeshift bed, not knowing
that woman, never having the opportunity
to see her on his weekend jaunts to the country
when she was always on her best behavior.

And there it stood in the air between us,
a small firm command with no hint of malice
that stiffened his shoulders and furrowed my brow.
Silence followed as we abandoned the sea
stitched in green and white, opting
for places of stolid separation.

Strings from the banjo and double bass
tuned in the summer air and old folks
gathered closer to hear endearing songs
from youths long gone. I felt inexplicably
ugly in the face of tenderness; always
pushing and pushing until bridges
collapse and I've no way home.

This Night

I won't sleep this night
out of worry that I'd be
faded in the hour you
need me most.

I let a cold breath
from the window blue
my toes like berries
in fear that warmth might
weigh heavy lids into slumber.
Instead, I allow the cat
to rub his face on them—
rest his downy white neck,
pulsating, on the ridge of digits.
He alerts me to reality.

I stare at the place you'd be
if this night found you close,
in arm's reach—head bowed
on a green couch, silent and safe.

Two dimensional ships set sail

His impatience with me is sometimes
notable as I wander off taking
photographs—finding worlds around
inanimate objects where he sees none.

Our point of views drastically askew,
his alive in the observation of the human
condition, mine static in the imprints
left behind by man and woman.

The vestibule of our sights
is seen from above and below
with our ages dictating the equations
of time and amassed energy.

There is a pinched tone in his voice,
biting tongue at me
always falling behind.

Side by Side Screaming

What happens when my voice cries out in the night?
Where does it go? Who catches it with their ear?

You sit there in quiet contemplation, a man
of so much silence reverberating

in your chest. You are a stone's throw,
a buzzing hummingbird's wing away

yet my body is frozen in fear of past
lover's taunts and heated rejections.

And I would have never imagined
you would be such a soft place to land

secretly wrapped in your own fears
until we lay side by side screaming

for courage and truth and resurrection
of faded hopes, once stunted dreams.

This time, this chance—I hear you.
We were bound to make it.

We Don't Get To Write The Ending

We get pulled from the wreckage
full of dog's teeth and returned letters.
The sender invisible and matriculated
into the paper. The holes in our arms
ooze venom and wickedness and words
you couldn't feed a baby.

You are there watching laundry
turn cyclical with an even huff and thump.

I sit in the dark watching the lights
on the tree fade in and out suspiciously
to the beating of my heart.

I am afraid to turn the lights out;
you are afraid to stop
the fragrant clothes from spinning.

It's here on the edges of reality
where we get bitten, sometimes maimed
in places no one can see.

So in all rights, we can say it never happened.
Denial is an easy shirt to wear;
truth a difficult word to swear.

In the end none of it matters.
            It is all recorded
in the disappearing ink
            of history.

The Window is Open

In the bathroom
I think my face
looks pretty, for once,
glowing on no sleep
and too much vodka.

I shut the light
and listened to the sounds
of the city at rest.

Standing at the door
I watch your ribs sleep
wishing for things I know

will never have viable
endings between your
rattled snoring
and my heart beating.

I slide my hand in yours,
whisper your name…
your ribs kept dancing
with the night.

My Lover

I feel a shadow of you
here, the pain drifting
quietly on the wind
tapping the glass
while I'm falling
asleep, uneasy and afraid.

I washed you
out of my pillowcases
to save myself the torture
of wondering why
with its faceless answers
that elude you often
and to save me
from wearing my own
hypocrisy like a smile.

Pain finds us in waves
of truth, roaring fierce
like our ocean,
finds us reluctant
to accept endings
in their finality,
keeps me optimistic
for open windows.

Your love filled more
crevices and hidden fortresses
on my body than I gave
it credit for. Those winds
ride through me uninhibited.
I am here unsure
of what a heart is supposed

to do; afraid to be forever
alone, afraid of having to settle
for less than you.

Another Lover Gone

When did I stop writing
poems about him, stop
loving him with more
than part of my heart?

Maybe I always knew
he'd be like the rest
or that I'd continue
to be myself—perpetually
unsatisfied and yearning
for the light just beyond
reach like the stranded
yellow of spring sunrise.

All this impossibility
shielded by hope
craving for security
with the truth speaking
itself in the metered
letters of my name
with me turning Van Gogh's
missing ear in its direction.

It is over now,
settled and complete
in its honest betrayal,
as if it never existed
and the evidence is only
apparent in the things
left behind.

Someone once said silence is golden

I put the pillow
to my face and inhale
what is left of you
until I feel as if I might
suffocate in your reality.

Time and space are cruel
injunctions and delirium seeps
in undetected like lucid dreaming.

I cannot tell visions from the truth.
I cannot define truth to discern visions
and I know I am not yet asleep
by the sound of sleet tapping at the window.

I put the pillow
over my face again
rebuilding you cell by cell
beside me. Your heat and flesh
and choking breath another dimension
and me frantic to learn
the physics needed
to find you between
the fibers of cotton
covering my senses.

Southern Cross

The moon is crescent,
north star close to earth and horizon
hovering over rooftops and telephone wires.

Two empty chairs
and an ashtray at capacity
are my company, lungs so drenched in smoke
it is a wonder I can breathe at all.

She told me she dreamt
we were together again,
and I quickly squashed the idea,

but you have been on my mind
as always, through it all,
and even high, I cannot shake
the thought of your hands on me.

I feel third wheel here, literally,
thinking it is maybe situational
while contemplating a self-imposed loneliness.

Hearts were played like decks of cards,
tossed around for no reason, or because
happiness scares the shit out of me,
denounces my capability to forge through.

The night rolls in colder and darker now
fresh on the skin, diabolical and twisted
like this life.

I Know

I know you went to our beach,
the snow piled high and thick,
where our summer once lay
hot and sweating.

I know you are yelling into the icy
wind, screaming from the jetty
with its rocks tattooed with razors
and you with open skin.

I know you went there with a fistful
of pride and sadness and hatred
feeling the rawness of life and
somehow making it a scar

rather than a badge.
There were tears left
in frozen sand like diamonds
that some child will mine

when the gulls fly circles
over their heads as they bend
digging for treasures and shells
and not worrying about the future.

I know you are biting at ghosts
and how they slip through your fingers
like air; biting the wounds you never
let heal with time and patience.

You always ask why, why, why
with no mountain for it to echo
off of and you are left there

alone by your own design.

I know I am kissing your face
while you are sleeping.

I know I am standing here
with a bruised heart, waiting.

I know I am.
I know you are.
I know we are still we.
I know.

Swimming in Dream

In your bed I lay,
my child's arms akimbo
over my body,
staring at the street light
dancing on the wall.

I hear the TV in the next
room, or maybe the computer,
and try to siphon the noise
out of my head. There must
be sleep for me somewhere
in this sea of black.

And swimming in dream,
you're there in another time,
perhaps another season,
and you are playing keeper
of the peace while I
mitigate unrest. You defend
what can only be
shared honor wrestled by spirit.

You didn't trust me with your life

I think about leaving
parts of you in the desert
to dry up and blow away

to let the sun bake you
into the earth
and make lighter

the air
between
us.

This wide open space
rumored to hold anything
that could fall from my mouth

before it evaporates
but I don't believe it.
There are lies hidden

in the sharp leaves
of the yucca. We created
blood pacts years ago.

My heart
knows where
I left my soul

on those cold nights
whispering to stars
who waited to burn

me in their shimmering
light, to quiet me.
I want to bury you

under the mission's cross,
let you suffer that wandering
feeling, no better than

tumbling
aimless in
the wind.

You'd know my heart
by the sound of its cry
and articulated memories.

It would be standing
naked beneath the mesquite,
needles bloodletting.

P

Vulpes

You must be open to everything, he tells me
as I walk out onto the porch to count stars
and burn lungs with the sweet south.

There is a great silence in noise
watching blue screened television through blinds,
and absorbing the hum of garage door lights
making a mirage on wet pavement. Rain trickles,
as if slow moving rivers, into the grate.

Water dripping from the wood beneath my feet
vibrates like the inner sanctum of a clockmaker,
the gears in my head constructing time stealers.

I hear 18 wheels on the wet curves, air in brakes
signaling the solemn fact that these small towns
go ghost on Sunday's at six. All that is left
are the strangers gliding over tangles of highway,
silver-backed foxes low slung in hunt.

With nimble fingers, even in the damp coming winter,
I tell him sadly, but with conviction,
There are no stars tonight, no stars.

He wanted a love poem

you can never undo that imprint
i lifted from the fibers of your
mind, those intricate wires
nestled in your nerve centers
whose electricity never failed
to defibrillate me whenever
you came close.

i wanted to whisper these things
behind your ear, let them grow
there like untended wildflowers
but i knew you would weed
them out in disbelief—your heart

empty like this watering can.

My Mouth is Full of Cliches

I am a beveled frame
around the angles
of your unscripted body.

There are wars going on
inside you as you realize
every Caesar has its Brutus

throughout history
no matter how small
you think you are.

And here you have been
poisoned with uncertain
failure clouded in regrets

you can't quite put your finger
on. Life is illusive in spite
of everything we can know.

This is the way
it goes.

Speaking in Tongues

He is a new vocabulary,
a litany of words,
that never pass my lips
but crest on the pure
undulation of my skin.

What sound falls
from the air
pushed violently
out of lungs?

How muscles ripple
beneath pressure
and understanding—
body leaves body
mind floats backwards

speaking in tongues,
gibberish,
fluent in
submission.

Music is a Systemic Fire

There are regions in the heart
I never travel anymore.
My blood slipping from atrium
to ventricle and then in reverse
so automatically I never feel
when it slows and pools, clotting
the awareness of the world.

I'm upright in my doorway
strumming my individual heart strings
hoping another recognizes the melody;
hoping they sense the vibration
that runs the ecosystem
of our shared form, but I never
can be sure in the end.

My fingers are calloused in some places
and raw in others when I stray
from the beat, performing the same song
over and over again.
I keep playing and yearning
and circulating blood
systematically waiting
to be noticed.

This is a beautiful line

"we all need to feel
like a bird on fire"

he whispered into
the crook of my knee
inhaling the perfumed
skin I was reborn
with—smoky and full
of flamed earth.

he traced the universe
on the back of my leg,
watched my ribs float
and stutter when a super
nova started to form,
spreading out like the fire
that brought me to him.

I felt the ashes
of my other life
painting my face, his face
our hands muddied
with ink and detritus;
our connection deeper
than the galaxy we
created on the tail
ends of breathing.

A Poem for the Lost Poems

At the rim of sleep
I squander the words
scrawled in pencil—
a gossamer transmutation
of fingers to paper
as I walk a dirt road.

It winds through
a trailer park
and I know then:

this is where
all the lost
poems go.

They are confined
in aluminum boxes
with dirty windows

unrecognizable
screaming
clawing at the door

a neglected dog.
All these moments
wasted in the Elysian Fields

where lucidity is impotent
and reality is the arbiter
of this mental gaping mouth.

We are all golden children

By candlelight, chaos
is dismantled within.

The golden shine of wooden
prayers penetrates deep

with hands folded together;
holding us together

with invisible strings
warm like morning sun.

Morning sun through leaves,
full of summer's riches,

baby in stroller, cooing
in wonder of the world

you are showing him
and will continue to share

whispering "we are all connected,
we are all golden children."

My Love is Five Sided

The room is dark
save a lone light shining
down from the silk veil
anchored to the ceiling.

It flutters when the door
opens, when I breathe in;
when the swaying of my body
becomes too much to hide.

The TV screen screams
like an eye as the transparent
silver pentagons wind together
in a helix at near imperceptible

speeds. I am frozen here—
incapacitated with a sudden
overwhelming need to be next
to you, your hand slipping gently

into mine to keep me from falling
at a rate so slow you couldn't
see it with the naked mind, only feel
it in the pulse at my wrist.

I am not sure how long
I've stood here with your phantom,
only warming one half of my existence,
not sure how long I will let my heart

pump through this
unattainable moment
    unattainable life

unattainable breath
    unattainable smile
before stepping away less of a woman.

Our existence is an epic poem

These things pass in the night—
lightning and frog song
the moth buzzing in the lamp
pride and failed hearts.

And it is all space
encompassing atoms
we cannot hold onto;
atoms we cannot realize

with the breadth of our minds.
We rely on form and function
to tell us how human
we are at each second.

We falter in long silences
afraid of implications.

We falter in the past
and its invisible grip.

These things pass in the night—
forgiveness and understanding
the shuttering leg of a cat
lost in dreaming.

You Can't Take It With You When You Go

He shouted
"Fuck you moon!"
and we laughed

standing in the cold
waiting for spring
to show her face.

In moments our bodies
would particulate
into their atoms

and the world would
cease to exist, reality
the dream we'd dream,

if we dreamt at all
floating to the ceiling
of the universe.

Shush

The only constant
is change, you tell me

and this pulls at my heart
its truth unprecedented

in a time when the mind
fumbles forward

on sugar kisses
and dragonflies in sun,

both imagined,
and the tiny girl within

wails knowing
she is really a woman

succumbing to silence
that is invariably
expected.

M

I Dare You

He warned against temptations
so she double dog dared him.

He returned with disbelief
so she pulled out the third dog

and dared him with that too.
She waited for his tongue to freeze

to the pole. They stood there
in opposite worlds armed to the teeth

with insanity and laughter
precipitated by love and all

its unpredictable mysteries.
They'd be together without question.

They'd risk their emotional savings
on a long shot that felt like a sure thing.

As the sun came up there was silence
in the receiver, in the room

that said more than any string
of words mouthed in repetition.

Your Flesh is 3,000 Miles Long

It's 4 in the morning
the filament in the lamp
is buzzing a lullaby
on the verge of compulsion
that only leads to darkness.

Your voice trickles
down the sides of my cheeks;
vibrates the inner workings
of my ear until I'm dizzy
and falling off the edge.

My mouth curls up
in a quiet smile,
a recognition that
I'm more alive than I
have ever been before,

remembering your sheepish
laugh and every time you made me
giggle from deep inside my belly.
Through the wires, I can see
your face soften and pulse race.

It is all I have
to fight back
the cold air
pushing in
from the cracks.

Continental 1551

I pace baggage claim
awaiting his arrival
riddled with anxiety
over the fact he'd
never make it
in one piece
or
at
all.

Behind me the sky
moves tumultuous
full of brevity
and quiet dissonance.
Cars creep like an army
of ants finding loved ones
lips
to
lips.

These smiles on faces
of long-losts peel
against the smell
of exhaust and jet fuel.
The pages of Marquez
turn silently with images
left
flat,
empty.

I see nothing
but the fire of his
eyes, this the only

light in the air I can
conjure, the cut of
his jaw in smile
the only angle I can
bear to create
without mathematical
calculations as my fingers
shake, pages falter
in their deserved
recognition.

I would walk
this street a thousand
years to see his face.

All the Glasses are Dirty

He sits there
drinking whiskey
from a coffee cup
staring off into
the distant
hills shrouded
in blue
and
I know
he must be
thinking
of his grandpa,
about life
repeating itself
in subtle ways.
The lines
around his
eyes say
this is true.

Black Licorice

In the candy aisle
we reminisced
about our separate
childhoods, how like music,
these sweets marked
milestones in the grooves
of our teeth, the cavities
reminders of how good
it felt to be young.

I grabbed the Necco wafers
and told you how my grandmother
always bought these,
the black licorice my favorite.

You stood there
suddenly child-like
and bright eyed
grabbing my face
in your hands,
kissing me.
All I could do
was smile.

Your Skilled Armies

The scales tip easily
in your favor,
a finger tracing
along the neck
a name whispered
low behind the ear
and you have won
the war before
fighting a battle.

My sudden arrest
an inward feeling
extracted by the insurgence
of your skilled armies
taking what you want,
turning every stone
over the tongue
and teeth
until my will
is broken beneath you.

Crusaders

In the morning
I find you stretched
across the expanse
of our bed.

Your eyes soft-lidded,
lips parted as if speaking
dreams now written
on exhaled breath.

I watch you
from the door,

passion rising up
from my toes.

My desire to engulf you
always palpable,
always tangible
at my fingertips.

I never bring myself
to disturb your peace.
I kiss the cross on your arm
believing silently
in the power of unnamed gods.

Haymaker

He taps the keys
hard like a war
is being fought
between his fingers
and synapses.

The repetition
of his words
drip guttural
and swing like
a haymaker
across the room.

Against the hum
of the refrigerator
I can hear nothing
but these mantras—
these hauntings
of creation
I've nothing
to do with.

Well Below Our Feet

To the sounds of highway
and children's laughter
he reads me poems
into the air feigning
a summer memory
we never shared.

His voice baritone
and sifting another man's
words from the page,
cigarette burning filter
between his fingers,
my heart racing.

I close my eyes to listen
our life still dream-like
wanton
comfortable
setting my brain on fire
with all possible angles
of love that moves deeper
than the core of earth
well below our feet.

I can tell when he looks at me
the words richer and louder
vibrating in the space around
my face as I stretch out full
in the porch chair.

When he is done
I secretly wish
for another—

want this French-made film
to continue

but he sits silent
staring at me.
His eyes have turned blue
under this sky
I used to call mine, alone,
the golden ring of desert
still burns in the center
and all I want to do
is feel his lips on mine
to taste the words
lingering there.

There is nothing left to wish for

I dared you
to stick your tongue
to the icy flagpole
inside my heart
never thinking
it'd work much better
than the Sunday horoscope.

Months feel like minutes
on the verge of decades.
Each day a discovery;
a new world I'd never
considered before seeing
the sharp angle of your face.

I've been captured
by your smile,
divided into a million
particles of light
by a heart bigger
than should be allowed
in one man's chest.
There is nothing
left to wish for.

For However Long That Might Be

We awake in the early afternoon
when the last evidence of morning's existence
creeps through the covered windows.

The damp breeze lifts the blinds
and taps them against the sill.

He rolls halfway over, back still facing me
and tells me he dreamed I sent him back to California
because of his allergies; he says I hand delivered him
to the airport to be sure he was gone.

There couldn't be anything further
from the truth but I suppose this is what
dreaming is for, expelling fears
and bridging disconnects.

We sit up against the pillows,
the room filled with the smell of sleep
until he lifts the blinds and lets in the spring.

The light rain pools water in the road
and the tires of cars make a familiar sound
as they move through them—a sound so comforting
I can never seem to describe it.

I finish a book about grief listening to these sounds
mixed with his breathing and the smell of his skin
drifting on the air through the screen.

These moments I have taken for granted
believing they will always be here when I want them,
but I know how life works, how it renders down the fat

and leaves us with little left to taste.

I want to tell him this, want to whisper in his ear
how lucky I am to know him for however long that might be,
but the moment passes and the domestic nature of our day
begins, something no less wonderful, but distracting.

It would leave the sentiment out of place
and he'd worry I was sad, so I just smile as he leaves the room,
still happy to know him, for however long that is, in secret.

Ghost of Another Woman

The eve of an ending intermingles itself
with new concepts you didn't anticipate
like family and the love of a ten year old.

We fish the pond from a triangulation
of points—our individual honey holes quiet,
and I see into your silence
standing with pole in hand
waiting for a solid bite.

The thoughts of the life you left behind
swirl around your head like flies
and your struggle to be present
never more evident.

I stay off into the distance
not wanting to see how much
it hurts you to think of her,
not wanting to go into battle
with the ghost of another woman.

Another Dinner Before Work

At the table,
we eat ham steak
and discuss religion,

how most people
are cowards for cursing
their gods or not believing
in them at all.

I admire your knowledge
that spans cultures
while I sit with my small ocean
of understanding contained
in a grain of sand.

The cat weaves between our legs
like thread, binding us together,
and we know he only pretends
to love us until something
better comes along.

Moon and Cigarette Smoke

We snuck away from the camp
under the guise of needing
to use the restroom.

The moon was full and shone
on the road so brilliantly
we left our flashlights
dead in our hands.

At the playground we moved
around like children—
the new-fangled teeter totter,
the swings and hanging loops
our bodies wouldn't fit through,
enticed us.

On the swings, we shared a smoke
and you told me how your mother
was the highest swinger you had ever seen.

I thought about my own special moments
on the swings with my mom but left it silent,
let your story live there in the moonlight
and cigarette smoke.

The Wisdom of Johnny Cash

Lying in bed
with you standing beside,
the small fan chilling your bare arms
as you tell me 25 things
most don't know about Johnny Cash.

Five whiskeys in
you can't remember most of
them either except the one about how
he painted his elevator after June died
and the fact that he never wanted
to be labeled as anything other
than a Christian when it came down to it.

We talked for hours
about religion and faith. About how
important it is to believe in something but in reality
so many have too much pride to believe in anything.
We shared some silence around the understanding
that we weave in and out of a shared circle—sometimes very alone
in our journeys, but still together.

Later in the hall, with the house clattering in silence,
the smell of your skin and the strength
of your arms made perfect sense.

Sleep is for the Lucky

From the doorway as I am drying my hair before bed
he tells me good luck as if I'm off to a big interview
or ready to scale an impossible fear.

I love that he thinks sleep is something for the lucky.

He knows it is a learned condition
for innate insomnia and OCD minds in recovery;
minds learning the art of doing nothing
which in reality is harder than one thinks.

He smiles because he knows he is clever
and then kisses me before he goes back out
into the rain to rip gnarled stumps from the ground.

Good luck, I think, we're going to need it.

You are a Mad Scientist

You are a mad scientist at the keyboard
with fingers punching distinctive rhythms
punctuated by classical violins
and the sound of my sewing machine
whirring forward and back.

Underneath is the faint breathing of words,
the turning of your mind finding calm
amidst a storm of memories and thoughts.

Outside the sun decides to shine
and the groan of a transmission
pushes through the window
as it trudges up our sharp angled hill.

I think to myself
we have made it
out of the dark holes
we were thrown down.

I think to myself,
we are home.

Laced with Regret

In the alley for silence and a smoke
my lungs say I shouldn't have
but my head says feels so good,
I let the dark spring night cover me.

These days I feel alone
and it can't be helped.

It's better than falling asleep
on the couch and seeing your face
in the morning laced with regret
knowing my feelings live at arm's length.

Painted Glass and the Meaning of Life

We walked to the museum in perfect weather.
It felt like an eternity since we'd shared
something simple, but important.

Five years looming on the horizon
and I've forgotten who I was before you arrived.

I contemplate the significance of this
in the grand scheme of life.

Have I lost myself?
Have we grown too comfortable?
What does that even mean?
But I say nothing.
Live in this moment, I tell myself.

We look at sculptures in the white, stark wing
and comment on pieces we love revisiting,
take note of new specimens.

The painted, hazy glass catches my attention.

I am alone in front of it, my body a blur in the center.
I feel lost in the world. You come and stand beside me,
the blur gets larger and changes shape.

It is something new. The piece is new, we are new.
I take our picture, *a portrait,* I say. You half smile
and say nothing.

I am home.
I am where I am supposed to be.

Thank You for Setting Me Free

Years have passed and I've clawed
my way out of the dark well,
fingernails broken and bleeding.

I blamed you for convincing me
to love again when I had given up.

I blamed you for the way you pretended
to be the only one, with your white-toothed smile,
and fingers crossed behind your back.

Now, the light on my face is brighter
than it's ever been, love bigger
than its four vessels can contain.

B

Submission as a Silent Survival

Obsessive
and consuming
the ebb and flow
of an entire life

built on the dichotomy
of being the object
of desire
and believing
its truth

Transfer of scents
from skin to skin
rising up
to overwhelm
at inappropriate
moments
like wearing
a dark memory

the blushing,
the heave of the breast,
heart rabbiting
in the chest
like wildfire
burning us up
to floating ashes
against the storm.

Kiss Me Before You Fall Asleep

"You write your name on things," he says.

"It's so I don't forget who I am. It's my weakness."

"They will sniff you out, you know...circle in
and attempt to exploit you. This is the truth."

"I know," I say, "my heart has been stabbed a million times."

"You have a big heart."

"With so many holes."

"You are stronger than you give yourself credit for."

"Maybe," I say, and lean back into the silence.

"No maybes"

"But they're so comfortable. The space the maybes live in is fluid
and changeable like the ocean pulling at the sand."

"The tide pulling at the sand is definitive and inevitable change," he
says quietly,
"a natural process that rearranges and shapes the moment,
the geography very gradually."

"It's subtle like a whisper."

"Not all whispers are subtle...some inflammatory and divisive."

"Like the ones you wish I'd spill into your ear?
You like a naughty whisper, I can tell."

"Yes," he says, "hell yes."

Philosophy

We live in video feed.
Smiling like teenagers
wondering how we got
so silly so fast.

He giggles,
    I giggle back.

This goes on for hours
sprinkled with philosophical discussion,
minds whirling and jumping from topic to topic.

There is silence too,
comfortable and sweet.

There is a heartfelt oneness
driven by friendship
and the memory of touch
sunken into fingerprints.

What we have isn't spoken
but lilts in the eyes.
Reality enough to make
the days long
as they orbit
around the sun.

Singular Virtue

He looked at me
through the screen
head tilted
in contemplation.
What he wanted
to tell me
hanging precariously
on the curve
of his bottom lip.

A deep sigh.

Nevermind, he said,
I don't want
to scare you.

I didn't push him.

That confession
on my own lips, waiting.
Patience has always been
my singular virtue.

The Definition of Synchronicity

By the light of individual screens,
faces in half lights
edged in shadows,
we touch each other
as if in dream.

Our fingers move
instinctively
across our bodies,
note breaths
and bites
and skin whispers.

"I want you here," he says,
"Your breasts on my chest
and your teeth on my neck."

I have nothing to say
because he's said it all.

Our bodies
undulating
like waves
being pulled to shore,
the definition
of synchronicity.

Unconcealed

Naked in the bathroom
I trace the bruise
in the shape of his thumb
near my knee
where he held
my leg down hard
to prevent my hips
from meeting his.

He wore a half smile
as I gasped
knowing I liked it
more than anyone
could imagine,
the domination
of wills my deep desire;
being held accountable
in the moment.

What We Don't Say

We've spoken of love
    its abstract nature
    its subjective hold

We've danced around
our separate pains
and encumbered truths

We've touched each other
in ways foreign to our skin
for so long and smiled

We've sparred in the living room
shadowboxing demons
both named and unnamed.

I think of how absence
makes the heart grow fonder
and not said it aloud

fearing we'd have to call
ourselves gay to play
it off to the side.

Our distance keeps
us whole and real
and wanting more

gives us freedom
to make scars
of fresh wounds.

Words of Infidels

Show me the places
the light has not seen
in a while; the secrets
hidden in silk spun skin
waiting to be discovered.

Inch by inch
a story whispered,
breath across the ear,
fingers tracing old wounds
and making them whole
with the words of infidels.

Unwound
    shaking
        lifting the body
            weightless and cursing gods
                we don't believe in.

Love is a No Contact Sport

Awkward face to face
words spilling out
as stutters echoing
the gap of a canyon

Speaking, comfort body,
fluidity, catch of eye
all outdated technologies
in the game of love

Screens and flying fingers
head bent, close together
so damn far away.

The Lost City

Our bodies are yoked together
with invisible tendrils
and delicate asters.

The sun takes its leave
and with it our connection
to relativity and matter.

Night dew settles on skin,
bare as the start of existence,
and tethered to a dream.

The Skylight

At my neck, he lingers,
lips enrapt in my heartbeat
pulsing like waves in the ocean.

I whisper something inaudible
vibration buzzing skin
and launching ships to space.

Your voice is a vision
      he says
I can see your heart
      he says

You won't love it when you're close
      I say
no one ever does
      I say

Who
understands words
Anymore?

Unified State of Cosmic Consciousness

Your touch blooms on my arm
with hesitation and hunger,
bleeding together like long lost friends
ready to smooth out differences
collected over time.

The look on your face,
eyes quizzical and pleading,
our skins barely together,
tell me you don't believe
I am real, only an apparition.

For unknown reasons,
this tenuous moment between us
builds a lust inside me
that rises up my center of gravity
and waits for your next move.

The Language of Flowers

In the blue light of a computer screen
I'd pretended to be asleep
while you held my foot, crying.

There were unspoken atrocities
bleeding through the layers
of your pajamas,

secrets you didn't have the courage
to share, knowing in the end, I'd be
just as fickle as the rest.

Those nights in the dark, with me falling
between the makeshift mattresses,
I thought your touches were the language
of flowers.

I remembered all of their parts
disarticulated in your mouth,
whispered into my spine

with a wholeness that neither
of us could remember enough
to make it tangible.

And then at the airport,
I told you I loved you
as I walked away, jets drowning

out the words. You paused,
as if knowing, back stiffened
and shoulders rolled down
as I flew away.

Flashes In the Pan

Ishmael

I had come from the East
with all things West new to me.
The weather, the scenery and the people
all strange and beautiful.
Ishmael was the most beautiful of all.
He sat behind me in the 4th grade
and I had to control myself
to keep from turning in my chair
to look at him, my body electric
just to be so near to him.

His skin was dark from the sun,
his black hair glinted.
Most of all I liked his smile
with the two silver front teeth
that captivated me.

He and his friends picked on me
at recess daily, they called me "Toro"
as I ran down the grass bank
after them, chasing them,
doing embarrassing things
to gain Ishmael's attention, his affection,
to think for one moment that
I was liked by them,
but all I really got
was a reputation
as a loco white girl.

Bound

We sat across from one another
in the lush grass of summer,
our legs folded Indian style
with knees so close
I could feel the heat of your skin.

You talked into the shadows
with your face barely visible
and your voice trailing in the air,
delicate and tenuous still
like a spider web.

I wanted to reach out to you
to cradle your face
in my hands,
to touch your lips
with my fingertips.

I am enraptured
by the sound of your voice,
bending my will
with the ideas of consequence,
and fulfilled destiny.

Each word implying
our meeting was not born
of circumstance,
or of chance,
but planned on a higher level,

And though our paths
have crossed
we remain bound
to different
Directions.

Collections

It is after work
and we smell
of hamburgers,
of old grease
as you back me
up in the darkness
to the edge of my bed.
The shade on the window
is only half drawn
with rays of street light
daggering on the wall.
I had wanted you
since the day you started,
had smiled my best smile,
batted my eyelashes,
whispered dirty things
when our arms crossed
over the warming table
for a double cheeseburger.
But now with you here,
in my room,
on my bed
touching me with a
drunken tenderness.
I don't find you
as attractive
now that the hunt is over;
Now that I have slain
the dragon,
but I let you touch me
anyway,
let you taste my skin,
let you slide inside me

just for the memory of it
as I tilt my head back,
and tilt my hips in
to collect my reward.

Fixations

I step off the bus
into the shadiest part of town,
with you flashing
your perma-grin
white against the night,
a hint of Cheshire
layered in your voice
as you pull my hand.

I feel loose and ragged,

un-cohesive at best
as we walk a block
I would never tread
in the daylight,
but you coax me into
doing things I have
no courage to do alone.

I turn to ask you
why the hell we're here,
but you leave me
alone on the bench
skirting the park,
used condoms littered
at my feet,
unknown liquids
crusting to the wood.

I slide my hands

into my lap listening to
hookers hanging in the shadows

sounds of oral fixations
and penetrations that
sneak up on me, not unlike
you as your hand slides
across my mouth, wet lips
spilling your devil in my ear,
on my neck
giving me the answer.

Jumping the Median

He always takes me places
I don't fit into.

Tonight, I find myself
in the local biker bar,
everyone hopped up on coke,
except me.

I drink my beers in the corner
pretending to like the music,
thinking about how infinitely
different the world
looks as the minority.

I am lost in this place
until he decides he's had enough
of watching me squirm
from across the smoky room.
He grabs my hand
pulling me hard as we run
across the four-lane highway,
jumping the median

it almost costs me
my life

but now my heart
is racing.

I am wet
with excitement

at cheating death
again.

We walk down the alley
behind Blue Video in an edgy
silence. He pushes me
against the wall, pinning
me with one arm, pushing
the air from my heaving chest
in the darkness, while the other
hand finds its way
down the front of my jeans.
His fingers slip in like a dream
and he smiles with conquest.

Ropes

My feet instinctively
follow the path
to his room.

In darkness,
flesh is bared
tentatively,

anticipating the burn
of his fingertips
on my skin.

I want him to take me,
then take me again.
I want to inhale him,

to devour him,
to swim in the waters
of his passion

under the haze of
this smoke screen
as his mouth tastes

the salt of my skin.

Joyride

He smells of coffee and cigarettes
as he grips the steering wheel,
one handed stiff armed, driving 80 mph
down the empty four-lane.

Windows rolled all the way down,
my hair a whirling dervish
in shuttered light of overhead lamps.
Our faces small pages of a flip-book
as our laughter dances around
long silences.

His desire to touch me,
kiss me, evident in the way
he leans into me around the sharp
curves of the highway; In the casual way
he misses my exit and smiles
from the side of his mouth.

I let him close enough to feel the heat
of his skin sweltering above the oppression
of this southern night, close enough
to keep him coming back for parts
of me he can never have.

Chanticleer

He called me effusive
beneath the neon
and streetlight glare,
my mind racing
to pin the definition
to the hanging word.

My eyes derailed
by his smile
and how his head
leaned against
the rooster wallpaper—
an endless succession
of fowl in summer touched colors.

The definition
still at a loss
between synapses
rippling as my voice
harvests accents from my youth
without warning, revealing
a lack of roots
and my inherent flitting nature.

I'm stunned
when his warm hand
wraps around mine
with an unforced silence,
calloused by wood,
tender with time.

Argentina

Your smile and that silver tongue
asking me to not make you
kiss me in the middle of the street.

In your truck, intoxicated sideways,
the lines of the road go by too fast
to remember where they started.

You said things I'd not heard
in far too long and I let myself
bathe in the words tumbling over
my warm, glistening flesh.

I didn't care if they were true
or if you'd remember my name,
only that it was possible to be alive again.

The First Four Songs Suck

He asks the bartender
for a napkin
pen scrawls fast
across it
left hand slant

He slides it across
the bar
use it or don't
whenever
you want.

I fold it in neat squares,
tuck it in the band
of my phone with a side smile.

I take the other half
of the napkin, right hand
Reciprocation.

The Rub

Five stools down
so much silence
protracted distance
between us when once
your hot breath pushed
into my ear, injected
with a deep need
I was supposed to fill

Now the stench of apathy
marches on pale wood
like an army of ants
carrying ten times
their weight, still strong.

Once I wanted you,
once you wanted me
and now, I just want
another beer.

Publication Notes

Some of the poems in this book were originally published online or in print in these fine magazines:

Amarillo Bay, Anti Heroin Chic, The Cartier Street Review, Burning Shores Press, Clutching at Straws, Debris Magazine, Fixator Press, Flutter, Gloom Cupboard, Gutter Eloquence Magazine, Heroin Love Songs, Indigo Rising, Litteratour, Literary Mary, Lunatic Chameleon, Motherkisser, Munyori Poetry Journal, Scythe Literary, Silenced Press, The Poetry Warrior, Writer's Bloc, Leaf Garden Press, MUST, Nibble, Roadside Raven Review, Wordsdance, Zygote in my Coffee, Alligator Stew, and Erbacce.

About the Author

Aleathia Drehmer is the creator and editor of *Durable Goods: The Missouri Collective* which featured poetry from high school students affected by trauma. She was once the editor of *In Between Altered States,* co-editor of *Full of Crow* and *Zygote in My Coffee,* and art editor of *Regardless of Authority.* Aleathia is the author of six chapbooks and currently has three collections of poetry available: *Running Red Lights* (Gutter Snob Books), *Looking for Wild Things* (Impspired), and *Layers of Half-Sung Hymns* (Cajun Mutt Press). She hosts open mic poetry readings at Card Carrying Books and Gifts in Corning, NY and had a Poetry in Play feature in May 2023 with the ARTS Council of the Southern Finger Lakes. You can follow Aleathia's journey at www.aleathiadrehmer.com

MORE ROADSIDE PRESS TITLES:

By Plane, Train or Coincidence
Michele McDannold

Prying
Jack Micheline, Charles Bukowski and Catfish McDaris

Wolf Whistles Behind the Dumpster
Dan Provost

Busking Blues: Recollections of a Chicago Street Musician and Squatter
Westley Heine

Unknowable Things
Kerry Trautman

How to Play House
Heather Dorn

Kiss the Heathens
Ryan Quinn Flanagan

St. James Infirmary
Steven Meloan

Street Corner Spirits
Westley Heine

A Room Above a Convenience Store
William Taylor Jr.

Resurrection Song
George Wallace

Nothing and Too Much to Talk About
Nancy Patrice Davenport

Bar Guide for the Seriously Deranged
Alan Catlin

MORE ROADSIDE PRESS TITLES:

Innocent Postcards
John Pietaro

Cistern Latitudes
James Duncan

Another Saturday Night in Jukebox Hell
Alan Catlin

Abandoned By All Things
Karl Koweski

Ain't These Sorrows Sweet?
Lauren Scharhag

Gregory Corso: Ten Times a Poet
Leon Horton, Editor

She Throws Herself Forward to Stop the Fall
Dave Newman

We Don't Get to Write the Ending
Aleathia Drehmer

These Many Cold Winters of the Heart
Ryan Quinn Flanagan

Things You Never Knew Existed
Josh Olsen

Green Roses Bloom for Icarus
Hiromi Yoshida

Let the Scaffolds Fall
Shaun Rouser

Apocalypsing
Jason Anderson